I0449593

St. Paul's Anglican Churchyard, Kingston, Ontario T - Z

The Grave Whisperer

Angeline Gallant

Published by Angeline Gallant, 2022.

ST. PAUL'S ANGLICAN CHURCHYARD, KINGSTON, ONTARIO T - Z

First edition. September 19, 2022.

ISBN: 978-1393084839

Written by Angeline Gallant.

Also by Angeline Gallant

Tell My Story: England 1852

The Grave Whisperer
Wedding Bells in Kingston, Ontario, Canada 1923
St. Paul's Anglican Churchyard Kingston, Ontario, Canada A-B
St. Paul's Anglican Churchyard, Kingston, Ontario, Canada C - D
St. Paul's Anglican Churchyard, Kingston, Ontario, Canada G - H
St. Paul's Anglican Churchyard, Kingston, Ontario, Canada J - N
St. Paul's Anglican Churchyard, Kingston, Ontario, Canada O - R
St. Paul's Anglican Churchyard, Kingston, Ontario, Canada S - T
St. Paul's Anglican Churchyard, Kingston, Ontario T - Z

The Wolf Whisperer Series
The Cry of the Wolf
Journey of the Heart
Wolf Whisperer volumes 1 & 2

Standalone
Winds of Change vol 1-3

Watch for more at https://www.goodreads.com/author/show/
19703964.Angeline_Gallant.

Table of Contents

GEORGE THUMWOOD[1]

G eorge passed away in 1819.
A church was built over his grave.

LIET-COL. FRANCIS SKELLY TIDY[2]

Francis was born in 1773.

He was 18 years old when the first parliament of Upper Canada assembled on September 17, 1791.

Francis was 42 years old when Napoleon Bonaparte was defeated in 1815.

He was 60 years old when the Factory Act was passed in 1833.

Francis was 64 years old when he passed away on October 9, 1837 and was buried on October 14th.

ABIGAIL TINDALL[3]

Abigail was buried on August 19, 1802.
A church was built over her grave.

SARAH TINDALL[4]

S arah was buried on August 30, 1802.
A church was built over her grave.

UNKNOWN TIPPADO[5]

They were only a child when they were buried on May 9, 1808. A church was built over their grave.

GERTRUDE TIPPER[6]

G ertrude was buried on August 25, 1805.
A church was built over her grave.

JAMES TIPPER[7]

J ames was buried on August 12, 1802.
A church was built over his grave.

MARIANNE TODD[8]

Marianne was born on May 13, 1844.

She was three years old when she passed away on April 21, 1848.

A church was built over her grave which is located beneath the parish hall.

MARY ANNE (PATRICK) TODD[9]

M ary Anne was born in Barking, England in 1782.
She was 33 years old when Napoleon Boneparte was defeated in 1815.

Mary was 53 years old when her mother passed away in 1835.

She was 61 years old when "A Christmas Carol" was first published in 1843.

Mary was 62 years old when she passed away on April 16, 1844.

A church was built over her grave which is located beneath the parish hall.

JAMES TORRANCE[10]

James was born in Scotland in 1779.

He was 22 years old when he married Elisabeth in Scotland in 1801.

James was 26 years old when his father passed away in 1805.

He was 36 years old when Napoleon Boneparte was defeated in 1815.

James was 38 years old when he passed away on September 10, 1817.

A church was built over his grave.

ELIZABETH TOSDEVINE[11]

E lizabeth was buried on February 15, 1808.
A church was built over her grave.

JOHN TREMIR[12]

John passed away in 1823.
A church was built over his grave.

CHARLES TRUMP[13]

Charles passed away in 1812.
A church was built over his grave.

JOHN TULLY[14]

J ohn was buried on November 5, 1802.
A church was built over his grave.

JAMES TURNER[15]

James passed away in 1811.
A church was built over his grave.

JAIRE UNDERUSHIN[16]

J aire was buried on September 11, 1809.
A church was built over the grave.

CATHARINE UNKNOWN[17]

C atharine was a slave before she passed away in 1811. A church was built over her grave.

INDE UNKNOWN[18]

Inde was listed as "A Negro woman" when she was buried on May 28, 1795.

A church was built over her grave.

PRINCE UNKNOWN[19]

P rince was listed as "A black man" when he was buried on May 16, 1806.

A church was built over his grave.

SOPHIA UNKNOWN[20]

Sophia was listed as "a black woman belonging to Mr. Robins" when she was buried on June 27, 1800.

A church was built over her grave.

MARY VALIERE[21]

Mary was buried on April 1, 1810.
A church was built over her grave.

JOSEPH VALLIER[22]

Joseph passed away in 1821.
A church was built over his grave.

FREDERICK WAGGONER[23]

F rederick was buried on September 9, 1803.
A church was built over his grave.

ELIZABETH WALKER[24]

E lizabeth was born in Manchester, England, in 1768.
She was 23 years old when the first parliament of Upper Canada assembled on September 17, 1791.

Elizabeth was 50 years old when she passed away on September 13, 1818. A church was built over her grave which is located beneath the parish hall.

HARRIET WALKER[25]

H arriet passed away in 1819.
A church was built over her grave.

MARTHA LOMAS WALKER[26]

Martha passed away in 1821.
A church was built over her grave

UNKNOWN WARD[27]

They were still a child when they passed away in 1816. A church was built over their grave.

JOHN M. WARD[28]

John was born in 1791 the same year that the first parliament of Upper Canada assembled on September 17th.

He was 28 years old when he passed away on September 13, 1819. A church was built over his grave.

CATHARINE ELIZABETH "CATHY" (WAYTE) WARWICK[29]

Cathy was born in Napanee, Ontario on November 29, 1947. She was seven years old when the General Motors auto workers went on strike in 1955.

Cathy was 34 years old when the Canada Act was passed in 1982.

She was 73 years old when she passed away on August 29, 2021.

UNKNOWN WASHBURN[30]

They were born in 1816 and passed away before December 1817. A church was built over their grave.

DANIEL WASHBURN JR.

D aniel was born in March 1815.
He was a year old when he passed away on September 6, 1816.
A church was built over his grave.

MARY (McLEAN) WASHBURN[31]

M ary was born in 1795.

She was 22 years old when she passed away on December 23, 1817.

A church was built over her grave.

LUCAS WATSON[32]

L ucas was buried on June 1, 1808.
A church was built over his grave.

REBECCA WATSON[33]

R ebecca passed away in 1818.
A church was built over her grave.

HENRY WERTELE[34]

H enry passed away in 1820.
A church was built over his grave.

JAMES WHITLOCK[35]

J ames was buried on August 26, 1804.
A church was built over his grave.

ISABELLA WILKINSON[36]

I sabella was born in November 1821.

She was four years old when she passed away on May 1, 1826.

A church was built over her grave which is located beneath the parish hall.

SARAH CATHERINE WILKINSON[37]

S arah was born in 1818.

    She was 10 years old when she passed away on February 7, 1828.

A church was built over her grave which is located beneath the parish hall.

SUSANNAH WILKINSON[38]

S usannah was born in 1830 and passed away that same year when she was 16 days old.

A church was built over her grave which is located beneath the parish hall.

WILLIAM WILKINSON[39]

William passed away in 1826.
A church was built over his grave.

ROBERT WILLIAMS[40]

R obert was buried on December 26, 1808.
A church was built over his grave.

JAMES L. WILLIS[41]

J ames passed away in 1818.
A church was built over his grave.

W. WILLIS[42]

They passed away in 1815.
A church was built over their grave.

CHARLES WILSON[43]

C harles was born in 1828.
He was three years old when he passed away on November 3, 1833.

A church was built over his grave which is located beneath the parish hall.

CHARLES WILKINSON WILSON[44]

C harles was born on January 3, 1840 in Kingston, Frontenac, Upper Canada, British Colonial America.

He was a month old when he passed away on February 18, 1840. A church was built over his grave which is located beneath the parish hall.

GEORGE ALFRED WILSON[45]

George was born in October 1830.

He was two years old when he passed away on June 27, 1833.

A church was built over his grave which is located beneath the parish hall.

JAMES HOLDITCH WILSON[46]

J ames was an infant when he passed away on April 17, 1844. A church was built over his grave.

JANE WILSON[47]

J ane was buried on December 21, 1807.
A church was built over her grave.

JOHN WILSON[48]

J ohn was buried on August 30, 1804.
   A church was built over his grave.

JOSEPH WILSON[49]

Joseph was born in Nunnington, England on October 12, 1810.

He was 30 years old when he passed away on February 8, 1841.

A church was built over his grave which is located beneath the parish hall.

MARY ELIZABETH (WILKINSON) WILSON[50]

M ary was born on June 25, 1819 in Kingston, Frontenac, Upper Canada, British Colonial America.

She was 20 years old when she passed away on January 13, 1840. A church was built over her grave which is located beneath the parish hall.

WILLIAM WILSON[51]

W illiam was buried on May 11, 1808.
A church was built over his grave.

WILLIAM WILSON[52]

William was buried on June 20, 1795.
A church was built over his grave.

PETER WITZEL[53]

P eter passed away in 1815.
A church was built over his grave.

"BABY" WOOD[54]

They were born in 1926 and passed away in 1927.

ELIZA WOOD[55]

E liza was buried on September 6, 1797. A church was built over her grave.

SOPHIA WOOD[56]

S ophia passed away on May 6, 1845.
   A church was built over her grave.

JARVIS WORDEN[57]

J arvis was buried on August 26, 1802.
A church was built over his grave.

JAMES WORKMAN[58]

J ames was buried on October 16, 1801.
A church was built over his grave.

JOHN WRIGHT[59]

J ohn passed away in 1788.
A church was built over his grave.

FRANCIS WYFOOT[60]

F rancis passed away in 1813.
A church was built over his grave.

MARIA YARWOOD[61]

Maria passed away in 1827.
A church was built over her grave.

WILLIAM YOUNG[62]

W illiam was buried on September 29, 1795.
A church was built over his grave.

[1] https://www.wikitree.com/genealogy/Thumwood-Family-Tree-12

[2] https://www.wikitree.com/genealogy/Tidy-Family-Tree-304

[3] https://www.wikitree.com/genealogy/Tindall-Family-Tree-1489

[4] https://www.wikitree.com/genealogy/Tindall-Family-Tree-1490

[5] https://www.wikitree.com/genealogy/Tippado-Family-Tree-1

[6] https://www.wikitree.com/genealogy/Tipper-Family-Tree-345

[7] https://www.wikitree.com/genealogy/Tipper-Family-Tree-346

[8] https://www.wikitree.com/genealogy/Todd-Family-Tree-12875

[9] https://www.wikitree.com/genealogy/Patrick-Family-Tree-6568

[10] https://www.wikitree.com/genealogy/Torrance-Family-Tree-668

[11] https://www.wikitree.com/genealogy/Tosdevine-Family-Tree-13

[12] https://www.wikitree.com/genealogy/Tremir-Family-Tree-1

[13] https://www.wikitree.com/genealogy/Trump-Family-Tree-667

[14] https://www.wikitree.com/genealogy/Tully-Family-Tree-1507

[15] https://www.wikitree.com/genealogy/Turner-Family-Tree-42806

[16] https://www.wikitree.com/genealogy/Underushin-Family-Tree-1

[17] https://www.wikitree.com/genealogy/Unknown-Family-Tree-619008

[18] https://www.wikitree.com/genealogy/Unknown-Family-Tree-619010

[19] https://www.wikitree.com/genealogy/Unknown-Family-Tree-619011

[20] https://www.wikitree.com/genealogy/Unknown-Family-Tree-619013

[21] https://www.wikitree.com/genealogy/Vali%C3%A8re-Family-Tree-24

[22] https://www.wikitree.com/genealogy/Vallier-Family-Tree-172

[23] https://www.wikitree.com/genealogy/Waggoner-Family-Tree-3059

[24] https://www.wikitree.com/genealogy/Walker-Family-Tree-60255

[25] https://www.wikitree.com/genealogy/Walker-Family-Tree-60256

[26] https://www.wikitree.com/genealogy/Walker-Family-Tree-60257

[27] https://www.wikitree.com/genealogy/Ward-Family-Tree-40197

[28] https://www.wikitree.com/genealogy/Ward-Family-Tree-40198

[29] https://www.wikitree.com/genealogy/Wayte-Family-Tree-134

[30] https://www.wikitree.com/genealogy/Washburn-Family-Tree-5583

[31] https://www.wikitree.com/genealogy/McLean-Family-Tree-10624

[32] https://www.wikitree.com/genealogy/Watson-Family-Tree-36121

[33] https://www.wikitree.com/genealogy/Watson-Family-Tree-36122

[34] https://www.wikitree.com/genealogy/Wertele-Family-Tree-1

[35] https://www.wikitree.com/genealogy/Whitlock-Family-Tree-2464

[36] https://www.wikitree.com/genealogy/Wilkinson-Family-Tree-14611

[37] https://www.wikitree.com/genealogy/Wilkinson-Family-Tree-14612

[38] https://www.wikitree.com/genealogy/Wilkinson-Family-Tree-14613

[39] https://www.wikitree.com/genealogy/Wilkinson-Family-Tree-14614

[40] https://www.wikitree.com/genealogy/Williams-Family-Tree-117008

[41] https://www.wikitree.com/genealogy/Willis-Family-Tree-14147

[42] https://www.wikitree.com/genealogy/Willis-Family-Tree-14148

[43] https://www.wikitree.com/genealogy/Wilson-Family-Tree-97996

[44] https://www.wikitree.com/genealogy/Wilson-Family-Tree-97997

[45] https://www.wikitree.com/genealogy/Wilson-Family-Tree-98001

[46] https://www.wikitree.com/genealogy/Wilson-Family-Tree-98002

[47] https://www.wikitree.com/genealogy/Wilson-Family-Tree-98003

[48] https://www.wikitree.com/genealogy/Wilson-Family-Tree-98004

[49] https://www.wikitree.com/genealogy/Wilson-Family-Tree-98006

[50] https://www.wikitree.com/genealogy/Wilkinson-Family-Tree-14616

[51] https://www.wikitree.com/genealogy/Wilson-Family-Tree-98007

[52] https://www.wikitree.com/genealogy/Wilson-Family-Tree-98008

[53] https://www.wikitree.com/genealogy/Witzel-Family-Tree-179

[54] https://www.wikitree.com/genealogy/Wood-Family-Tree-47668

[55] https://www.wikitree.com/genealogy/Wood-Family-Tree-47669

[56] https://www.wikitree.com/genealogy/Unknown-Family-Tree-619163

[57] https://www.wikitree.com/genealogy/Worden-Family-Tree-7385

[58] https://www.wikitree.com/genealogy/Workman-Family-Tree-4300

[59] https://www.wikitree.com/genealogy/Wright-Family-Tree-58101

[60] https://www.wikitree.com/genealogy/Wyfoot-Family-Tree-1

[61] https://www.wikitree.com/genealogy/Yarwood-Family-Tree-224

[62] https://www.wikitree.com/genealogy/Young-Family-Tree-54219

Don't miss out!

Visit the website below and you can sign up to receive emails whenever Angeline Gallant publishes a new book. There's no charge and no obligation.

https://books2read.com/r/B-A-QGSI-MCIBC

BOOKS 2 READ

Connecting independent readers to independent writers.

Also by Angeline Gallant

Calling Her Heart
Whisper of the Heart
No Turning Back
Forsake Me Not
Hear My Cry

Keeper Of Secrets
A Lady's Secret

Midnight's Awakening
Heart of the Storm
Walking Through The Storm

Secrets of the Underworld
Deklan's Dragons

Tell My Story Collection

Tell My Story: England 1852

The Grave Whisperer
Wedding Bells in Kingston, Ontario, Canada 1923
St. Paul's Anglican Churchyard Kingston, Ontario, Canada A-B
St. Paul's Anglican Churchyard, Kingston, Ontario, Canada C - D
St. Paul's Anglican Churchyard, Kingston, Ontario, Canada G - H
St. Paul's Anglican Churchyard, Kingston, Ontario, Canada J - N
St. Paul's Anglican Churchyard, Kingston, Ontario, Canada O - R
St. Paul's Anglican Churchyard, Kingston, Ontario, Canada S - T
St. Paul's Anglican Churchyard, Kingston, Ontario T - Z

The Wolf Whisperer Series
The Cry of the Wolf
Journey of the Heart
Wolf Whisperer volumes 1 & 2

Standalone
Winds of Change vol 1-3

Watch for more at https://www.goodreads.com/author/show/
19703964.Angeline_Gallant.

About the Author

Angeline Gallant is a Geneology addict who loves to work on her family tree and help others with theirs. This passion for history plays a huge role in her books as well.

An Old Stock Canadian and a homeschooling mother living in Canada, Angeline is determined to leave her own special mark on the world through her work, her child, and her writing.

Angeline is an author on Goodreads. If you follow her account on Goodreads, she will follow back.

Read more at https://www.goodreads.com/author/show/19703964.Angeline_Gallant.